About this Learning Guide

Shmoop Will Make You a Better Lover*
*of Literature, History, Poetry, Life...

Our lively learning guides are written by experts and educators who want to show your brain a good time. Shmoop writers come primarily from Ph.D. programs at top universities, including Stanford, Harvard, and UC Berkeley.

Want more Shmoop? We cover literature, poetry, bestsellers, music, US history, civics, biographies (and the list keeps growing). Drop by our website to see the latest.

www.shmoop.com

Table of Contents

Introduction

In a Nutshell

Sophocles is considered one of the great ancient Greek tragedians. Among Sophocles' most famous plays are *Oedipus the King*, *Oedipus at Colonus*, and *Antigone*. These plays follow the fall of the great king, Oedipus, and later the tragedies that his children suffer. The *Oedipus* plays have had a wide-reaching influence and are particularly notable for inspiring Sigmund Freud's theory of the "Oedipus Complex," which describes a stage of psychological development in which a child sees their father as an adversarial competitor for his or her mother's attention (or in non-psychology speak, it's the kill-the-father-sleep-with-the-mother complex).

The three plays are often called a trilogy, but this is technically incorrect. They weren't written to be performed together. In fact they weren't even written in order. *Antigone*, which comes last chronologically, was the play Sophocles wrote first, around 440 B.C. It wasn't until about 430 B.C that Sophocles produced his masterpiece *Oedipus the King*. He finally wrote *Oedipus at Colonus* in 401 B.C., near the end of his life. Also note that the plays were rarely if ever revived during the playwright's life time, so it's not like it would have been easy for Sophocles' audiences to compare them.

These facts probably explain some of discrepancies found in the plays. For example, while Creon is the undisputed King at the end of *Oedipus the King*, in *Oedipus at Colonus* it's Polyneices and Eteocles who are battling for the throne. In *Antigone*, Creon assumes the throne with no mention of the fact that he's ever sat on it before. It's pretty unlikely that Sophocles forgot this key fact. But it could very well be that it just didn't matter very much. Each play is a separate interpretation of the myth, not a part of a trilogy. Sophocles would've been under no obligation to make the plays coherent in every detail.

Of course, while the plays aren't technically a trilogy and do have discrepancies, they do share many similarities. Several of the key characters put in repeat appearances, including Oedipus, Creon, Teiresias, Ismene, and Antigone. Also, the plays have a lot of the same themes. The plays all deal in some way with the will of man vs. the will of the gods. Self-injury and suicide also plague the family until the end. It seems that Oedipus's family is never quite capable of escaping the pollution of his terrible mistakes.

Why Should I Care?

Antigone matters because it wrestles with civil disobedience. Remember how Ismene asks Antigone to just forget about burying their brother's body (which, according to the king's latest law, is an act punishable by death) and to instead marry the king's dreamy son and live happily ever after? Antigone isn't willing to forget her brother. She sees burying her brother as a moral imperative, which supersedes human-created laws. And she's not the only person who has courageously placed morals over state laws.

Reach into the depths of the history room in your mind. You have lots of modern examples of people who have chosen to fight for justice rather than preserve their own safety. Consider Dr. Martin Luther King, Jr. or Gandhi, both advocates of civil disobedience and peaceful demonstrations, who were assassinated as a result of their fights against oppression. Or think about Nelson Mandela, who risked years in jail to stand up against the apartheid government in South Africa.

Antigone chooses to express her dissatisfaction with what she believes to be the unethical new regime of King Creon by burying her brother's body. Antigone resolves to sacrifice her own life in the service of a greater justice. It's this kind of almost superhuman resolve that changes the course of history, and that's something that we can admire equally in the 5th century B.C. and the 21st century A.D.

Summary

Book Summary

Antigone picks up where *Oedipus at Colonus* leaves off. Oedipus has just passed away in Colonus, and Antigone and her sister decide to return to Thebes with the intention of helping their brothers, Eteocles and Polyneices, avoid a prophecy that predicts they will kill each other in a battle for the throne of Thebes.

Upon her arrival in Thebes, Antigone learns that both of her brothers are dead. Eteocles has been given a proper burial, but Creon, Antigone's uncle who has inherited the throne, has issued a royal edict banning the burial of Polyneices, who he believes was a traitor. Antigone defies the law, buries her brother, and is caught. When Creon locks her away in prison, she kills herself.

Meanwhile, not realizing Antigone has taken her own life, the blind prophet Teiresias, Creon's son and Antigone's fiancé Haemon, and the Chorus plead with Creon to release her. Creon finally relents, but in an instance of too-late-timing, finds her dead in her jail cell. Out of despair, Haemon and Creon's wife have by now also killed themselves, and Creon is left in distress and sorrow.

Antigone

- At the end of *Oedipus at Colonus*, Oedipus has passed away. Antigone, knowing that her brothers are waging war against each other in a battle for the throne of Thebes, decides to return to Thebes in order to prevent them from killing each other.
- When Antigone arrives in Thebes, she and her sister Ismene talk outside the palace gate, where we learn that their brothers, Polyneices and Eteocles, have indeed killed each other.
- Antigone is disturbed because Creon, who is now ruling, has ordered that Eteocles be buried with the formal rites, but that Polyneices be left unburied and unmourned.
- Anyone who buries Polyneices will be punished by death. That's what we call a "deterrent."
- Antigone intends to defy the law to bury her brother according to the wishes of the gods.

She asks if Ismene will help her.

- Ismene says she can't bring herself to do it. She feels that her family's consistently terrible luck and the fact that she's a woman are quite inhibiting.
- Antigone says she's willing to do it alone, and wouldn't mind dying in order to secure Polyneices's rightful burial.
- Ismene warns Antigone against fighting The Man. She thinks it's a losing battle.
- The Chorus explains the battle that transpired between Polyneices and Eteocles, with lots of useless details like who stuck whose sword where.
- Creon arrives and announces to a gathering that, whereas Eteocles behaved honorably in defending the city, Polyneices was a dishonorable exile. He offers this as an explanation for why Eteocles gets buried but Polyneices is left out for the birds.
- A sentry arrives. He's scared out of his mind at being the messenger of bad news, because sometimes these royal types can get quite aggressive.
- He still does his job and reveals to Creon that Polyneices's body has been ritually prepared.
- The Chorus chimes in that perhaps the burial was the will of the gods.
- Creon angrily responds that Polyneices spited the gods with his actions. Creon suspects that someone got paid off to break the law this way.
- Creon demands that the sentry discover who did it. He then threatens the poor sentry with death if he can't figure it out. Now we understand why the messenger was so scared about five minutes ago.
- The Chorus remarks on the strength and resilience of mankind. Really? Because we were remarking on how unfair the sentry's lot in life is.
- The sentry returns with Antigone in tow and announces that she was discovered burying Polyneices.
- Antigone does not deny that she committed the crime. (Go principles!) She explains that while she knew it was against Creon's edict, her actions were in line with her obligations to justice and the gods.
- The Chorus accuses Antigone of being inclined to trouble – just like her father.
- Creon says that he resents Antigone's moralizing and then vows to execute her. He summons Ismene, who he assumes is also involved.
- Creon attempts to shame Antigone for what he sees as her radical views. However, she remains determined and unshaken (also like her father).
- Antigone's general stubbornness forces Creon into an argument over whether Polyneices deserved the same burial as his brother.
- Ismene enters the room. She is questioned and says that she is guilty of having aided Antigone in the burial. (Go principles, again. Well, maybe.)
- Antigone insists that her sister not confess to a crime she didn't do. Ismene counters that she could not go on living without Antigone. (Go sisters.)
- It is revealed that Antigone is engaged to marry Creon's son, Haemon. Haemon apparently has some back up future wives in the wings or, as Creon says, he has "other fields to plow" (!). In short, his bed won't be lonely if Antigone dies.
- The Chorus laments life's sufferings. OK, NOW we're on the same page.
- Haemon arrives. He informs his father Creon that he will honor and obey whatever Creon decides about Antigone, which is either honorable (for respecting his father) or despicable (for letting his fiancée die).
- Creon lectures Haemon about the critical importance of the law and obedience. Haemon is

like, "Come on, Dad."

- Creon feels it's particularly important not to be beaten by a person of the female persuasion.
- Haemon responds that while he does not question his father's wisdom, he sees the city mourning Antigone's suffering, not to mention living in terror of Creon's wrath (think about the sentry). Haemon advises Creon to pay attention to popular sentiment and to be open to the advice of others.
- As the argument escalates, Haemon tells Creon he's insane and Creon tells Haemon he's a woman's slave. Ouch.
- Since there's no one around to put them in the time-out corner, they end things themselves.
- Haemon storms out, and Creon goes back to thinking about how to punish Antigone.
- The Chorus, apparently having given up on Antigone, tries to dissuade Creon from punishing Ismene, who clearly did not participate in Polyneices's burial.
- Antigone utters a cryptic line about marrying death. Yikes.
- As the Chorus muses, Teiresias (the blind prophet) arrives to speak with Creon.
- Teiresias advises Creon not to leave Polyneices unburied or to kill Antigone. Good old Teiresias.
- Creon scoffs at his advice and accuses Teiresias of seeking personal profit. This is sounding mighty familiar.
- Teiresias remarks that no one seems able to listen and hear good advice.
- Teiresias warns that Creon's unwillingness to bury Polyneices and permit Antigone to live will anger the gods and be reciprocated by his own death. Uh-oh.
- Teiresias leaves and the Chorus reminds Creon that he is never wrong. That is, *Teiresias* is never wrong. Please, Creon is wrong all the time.
- Creon grapples with his choices. At the Chorus's urging, he decides to release Antigone (yay) and see to Polyneices's burial (yay again).
- A messenger arrives and announces that Haemon has killed himself out of anger and despair at his father.
- Creon's wife, Eurydice, arrives and asks what's going on.
- The messenger recounts the series of events. Antigone hanged herself, and finding her there dead, Haemon attempted to strike his father with his sword. He missed, and then took his own life.
- Creon arrives, desperately regretting his mistake.
- A second messenger enters and informs the royal gang that more tragedy has struck.
- Eurydice, in despair over her lost son and enraged with Creon, took her own life.
- In despair and fear of his own death, Creon asks...to be killed? No. For pins to gouge out his eyes? No, not that either. He asks to be led off stage. Not really what we were expecting, but OK.

Themes

Theme of Fate and Free Will

A central theme of *Antigone* is the tension between individual action and fate. While free choices, such as Antigone's decision to defy Creon's edict, are significant, fate is responsible for many of the most critical and devastating events of the trilogy. By elevating the importance of fate, Sophocles suggests that characters cannot be fully responsible for their actions. It becomes difficult, for example, to blame Oedipus for marrying mother given his ignorance.

Questions About Fate and Free Will

1. Do some characters seem to control their fates more than others? If so, how do they do it?
2. How does Oedipus's fate impact the fates of other members of his family?

Chew on Fate and Free Will

Antigone is not limited by fate, rather by the knowledge of her fate.

Theme of Rules and Order

Antigone contrasts two types of law and justice: divine or religious law on one hand, and the law of men and states on the other. Because of the centrality of fate and the rule of the gods in the lives of the main characters of the play, religious rites and traditions are elevated to the status of law. While questions of law and justice play a role in all three plays of the *Oedipus* trilogy, they are most prominent in *Antigone*, in which Antigone's standards of divine justice clash with Creon's will as the head of state.

Questions About Rules and Order

1. To what extent is adherence to the law of the state associated with virtue? Adherence to divine law?
2. How compatible are divine and state law in *Antigone*? Where does conflict arise?

Chew on Rules and Order

Antigone's adherence to religious rites as divine law is as self-serving as Creon's creation of laws that serve his interests.

Theme of Determination

Determination is a nearly universal character trait amongst the cast of *Antigone*. Despite the important role of fate in the lives of the characters, Creon, Antigone, Ismene, and Polyneices are all driven, at times stubbornly, to pursue their goals. Determination in the play is linked to hubris and proves less an asset than a flaw to the characters that possess it.

Questions About Determination

1. To what extent is determination an asset to characters in *Antigone*? How is it a hindrance?
2. What, if any, correlation exists between determination and self-deception in the play?
3. Are all of the determined characters in *Antigone* stubborn and arrogant, or do some exhibit a reasonable degree of determination? What might this suggest?

Chew on Determination

Determination to seek, to know, and to pursue principle is depicted as tantamount to self-injury in the *Oedipus* trilogy.

Theme of Power

Power both corrupts and metaphorically blinds characters in *Antigone*. The clearest example of power is King Creon of Thebes, who is arrogant, unperceptive, and downright mean to people around him.

Questions About Power

1. How is Creon the Brother-in-Law (from *Oedipus the King* different from Creon the King?
2. Do women have positions of power in *Antigone* trilogy? If so, how do they exercise their power?

Chew on Power

In *Antigone*, power corrupts. When simply the King's brother-in-law, Creon was a reasonable man, whereas when he inherits the role of king, he becomes arrogant and cruel.

Theme of Women and Femininity

Antigone explores a contrast between the behavior expected of women and the reality of their role in society. Creon expects men to be the primary actors in society and women to take a secondary and subservient role. Opinionated Antigone challenges these notions as she takes center stage and presents formidable challenges to the men around her.

Questions About Women and Femininity

1. Discuss Ismene's perception of her role as a woman in ancient Greek society. Does her behavior match the opinions she voices?
2. Why does Creon feel so threatened by Antigone? Does this have anything to do with her womanhood?

3. Do Antigone and Ismene fulfill more stereotypically masculine roles than their brothers Eteocles and Polyneices?

Chew on Women and Femininity

Creon gives Antigone a harsh punishment simply because she is a woman; if the law-breaker had been a man, he would not have been sentenced to death.

Theme of Mortality

Self-injury and suicide are almost universally prevalent among the main characters in the *Oedipus* trilogy, and particularly in *Antigone*. Antigone, Haemon, and Eurydice each commit suicide; Polyneices and Eteocles willingly take actions that result in their deaths. The frequency of suicide and death more broadly suggest that in the context of the plays, life is tenuous, and that taking one's own life is an acceptable, if tragic, way of dying. Furthermore, self-injury and suicide seem to be the only ways in which characters in *Antigone* are able to influence their destinies.

Questions About Mortality

1. Why do some characters, such as Antigone, look favorably on death?
2. Why do Haemon and Eurydice kill themselves?

Chew on Mortality

Suicide in *Antigone* is a consequence of characters' frustration that they have no influence over their own fate.

Suicide in *Antigone* is employed by characters who accept and are at peace with their fate.

Suicide in *Antigone* is employed by characters who are trying to escape their fate.

Quotes

Fate and Free Will Quotes

ISMENE
I scorn them not, but to defy the State
Or break her ordinance I have no skill.
ANTIGONE
A specious pretext. I will go alone
To lap my dearest brother in the grave.
ISMENE
My poor, fond sister, how I fear for thee!

ANTIGONE
O waste no fears on me; look to thyself. (82-85)

Thought: While Antigone feels empowered to impact her own destiny, Ismene does not.

ISMENE
O sister, scorn me not, let me but share
Thy work of piety, and with thee die.
ANTIGONE
Claim not a work in which thou hadst no hand;
One death sufficeth. Wherefore should'st thou die?
ISMENE
What would life profit me bereft of thee?
ANTIGONE
Ask Creon, he's thy kinsman and best friend.
ISMENE
Why taunt me? Find'st thou pleasure in these gibes?
ANTIGONE
'Tis a sad mockery, if indeed I mock.
ISMENE
O say if I can help thee even now.
ANTIGONE
No, save thyself; I grudge not thy escape.
ISMENE
Is e'en this boon denied, to share thy lot?
ANTIGONE
Yea, for thou chosed'st life, and I to die. (544-556)

Thought: Antigone chooses both her own destiny (death) and her sister's (life). She demonstrates that there is such a thing as free will, after all.

CREON
I know it too, and it perplexes me.
To yield is grievous, but the obstinate soul
That fights with Fate, is smitten grievously. (1095-1099)

Thought: Although Creon wants to resist, he knows better than to fight fate. He has learned from Oedipus's mistakes.

Rules and Order Quotes

ISMENE
Bethink thee, sister, of our father's fate,
Abhorred, dishonored, self-convinced of sin,

Blinded, himself his executioner.
Think of his mother-wife (ill sorted names)
Done by a noose herself had twined to death
And last, our hapless brethren in one day,
Both in a mutual destiny involved,
Self-slaughtered, both the slayer and the slain.
Bethink thee, sister, we are left alone;
Shall we not perish wretchedest of all,
If in defiance of the law we cross
A monarch's will?--weak women, think of that,
Not framed by nature to contend with men.
Remember this too that the stronger rules;
We must obey his orders, these or worse.
Therefore I plead compulsion and entreat
The dead to pardon. I perforce obey
The powers that be. 'Tis foolishness, I ween,
To overstep in aught the golden mean. (49-68)

Thought: Ismene fears betraying the laws of state, whereas her sister is more concerned with divine law.

ANTIGONE
I urge no more; nay, wert thou willing still,
I would not welcome such a fellowship.
Go thine own way; myself will bury him.
How sweet to die in such employ, to rest,--
Sister and brother linked in love's embrace--
A sinless sinner, banned awhile on earth,
But by the dead commended; and with them
I shall abide for ever. As for thee,
Scorn, if thou wilt, the eternal laws of Heaven.
ISMENE
I scorn them not, but to defy the State
Or break her ordinance I have no skill. (69-79)

Thought: Antigone elevates religious law above the law of the state, while Ismene is more concerned with the laws of the state.

(Ant. 2)
Passing the wildest flight thought are the cunning and skill,
That guide man now to the light, but now to counsels of ill.
If he honors the laws of the land, and reveres the Gods of the State
Proudly his city shall stand; but a cityless outcast I rate
Whoso bold in his pride from the path of right doth depart;
Ne'er may I sit by his side, or share the thoughts of his heart. (368-375)

Thought: The Chorus explains that it is essential to honor both the laws of the land and of the gods.

CREON
And yet wert bold enough to break the law?
ANTIGONE
Yea, for these laws were not ordained of Zeus,
And she who sits enthroned with gods below,
Justice, enacted not these human laws.
Nor did I deem that thou, a mortal man,
Could'st by a breath annul and override
The immutable unwritten laws of Heaven.
They were not born today nor yesterday;
They die not; and none knoweth whence they sprang.
I was not like, who feared no mortal's frown,
To disobey these laws and so provoke
The wrath of Heaven. I knew that I must die,
E'en hadst thou not proclaimed it; and if death
Is thereby hastened, I shall count it gain.
For death is gain to him whose life, like mine,
Is full of misery. Thus my lot appears
Not sad, but blissful; for had I endured
To leave my mother's son unburied there,
I should have grieved with reason, but not now.
And if in this thou judgest me a fool,
Methinks the judge of folly's not acquit. (449-470)

Thought: Antigone challenges Creon's moral and legal authority by elevating religious rites above his worldly law.

HAEMON
The Theban commons with one voice say, No.
CREON
What, shall the mob dictate my policy?
HAEMON
'Tis thou, methinks, who speakest like a boy.
CREON
Am I to rule for others, or myself?
HAEMON
A State for one man is no State at all.
CREON
The State is his who rules it, so 'tis held.
HAEMON
As monarch of a desert thou wouldst shine.
CREON

This boy, methinks, maintains the woman's cause.
HAEMON
If thou be'st woman, yes. My thought's for thee.
CREON
O reprobate, would'st wrangle with thy sire? (734-742)

Thought: Haemon suggests that Creon's sense of justice is flawed.

ANTIGONE
The slain man was no villain but a brother.
CREON
The patriot perished by the outlaw's brand.
ANTIGONE
Nathless the realms below these rites require.
CREON
Not that the base should fare as do the brave.
ANTIGONE
Who knows if this world's crimes are virtues there? (515-523)

Thought: Antigone looks to divine law for justice, while Creon elevates his own notions of pragmatism and morality.

Determination Quotes

ISMENE
Bethink thee, sister, of our father's fate,
Abhorred, dishonored, self-convinced of sin,
Blinded, himself his executioner.
Think of his mother-wife (ill sorted names)
Done by a noose herself had twined to death
And last, our hapless brethren in one day,
Both in a mutual destiny involved,
Self-slaughtered, both the slayer and the slain.
Bethink thee, sister, we are left alone;
Shall we not perish wretchedest of all,
If in defiance of the law we cross
A monarch's will?--weak women, think of that,
Not framed by nature to contend with men.
Remember this too that the stronger rules;
We must obey his orders, these or worse.
Therefore I plead compulsion and entreat
The dead to pardon. I perforce obey
The powers that be. 'Tis foolishness, I ween,
To overstep in aught the golden mean. (49-68)

Thought: While not heroic, Ismene's determination to survive reveals her sound reason and powerful instinct for self-preservation.

ANTIGONE
I urge no more; nay, wert thou willing still,
I would not welcome such a fellowship.
Go thine own way; myself will bury him.
How sweet to die in such employ, to rest,--
Sister and brother linked in love's embrace--
A sinless sinner, banned awhile on earth,
But by the dead commended; and with them
I shall abide for ever. As for thee,
Scorn, if thou wilt, the eternal laws of Heaven. (69-76)

Thought: Antigone's enthusiastic determination to risk her life in order to bury her brother is suicidal in nature.

CREON
O cease, you vex me with your babblement;
I am like to think you dote in your old age.
Is it not arrant folly to pretend
That gods would have a thought for this dead man?
Did they forsooth award him special grace,
And as some benefactor bury him,
Who came to fire their hallowed sanctuaries,
To sack their shrines, to desolate their land,
And scout their ordinances? Or perchance
The gods bestow their favors on the bad.
No! no! I have long noted malcontents
Who wagged their heads, and kicked against the yoke,
Misliking these my orders, and my rule.
'Tis they, I warrant, who suborned my guards
By bribes. Of evils current upon earth
The worst is money. Money 'tis that sacks
Cities, and drives men forth from hearth and home;
Warps and seduces native innocence,
And breeds a habit of dishonesty.
But they who sold themselves shall find their greed
Out-shot the mark, and rue it soon or late.
Yea, as I still revere the dread of Zeus,
By Zeus I swear, except ye find and bring
Before my presence here the very man
Who carried out this lawless burial,
Death for your punishment shall not suffice.
Hanged on a cross, alive ye first shall make

Confession of this outrage. This will teach you
What practices are like to serve your turn.
There are some villainies that bring no gain.
For by dishonesty the few may thrive,
The many come to ruin and disgrace. (280-314)

Thought: Creon's fierce determination to prosecute the burier of Polyneices will ultimately lead to the suicides of his wife, son, and niece. Like Oedipus, his determination causes death.

CREON
Well, let her know the stubbornest of wills
Are soonest bended, as the hardest iron,
O'er-heated in the fire to brittleness,
Flies soonest into fragments, shivered through.
A snaffle curbs the fieriest steed, and he
Who in subjection lives must needs be meek.
But this proud girl, in insolence well-schooled,
First overstepped the established law, and then--
A second and worse act of insolence--
She boasts and glories in her wickedness.
Now if she thus can flout authority
Unpunished, I am woman, she the man.
But though she be my sister's child or nearer
Of kin than all who worship at my hearth,
Nor she nor yet her sister shall escape
The utmost penalty, for both I hold,
As arch-conspirators, of equal guilt.
Bring forth the older; even now I saw her
Within the palace, frenzied and distraught.
The workings of the mind discover oft
Dark deeds in darkness schemed, before the act.
More hateful still the miscreant who seeks
When caught, to make a virtue of a crime. (474-496)

Thought: Blind to his own stubbornness, Creon attacks and punishes Antigone for denying his authority and for her unwillingness to submit to his will.

ANTIGONE
Would'st thou do more than slay thy prisoner?
CREON
Not I, thy life is mine, and that's enough.
ANTIGONE
Why dally then? To me no word of thine
Is pleasant: God forbid it e'er should please;
Nor am I more acceptable to thee.

And yet how otherwise had I achieved
A name so glorious as by burying
A brother? so my townsmen all would say,
Where they not gagged by terror, Manifold
A king's prerogatives, and not the least
That all his acts and all his words are law. (497-506)

Thought: Antigone exhibits a self-destructive determination to sacrifice her life for principle.

Power Quotes

GUARD
May I not speak, or must I turn and go
Without a word?--
CREON
Begone! canst thou not see
That e'en this question irks me?
GUARD
Where, my lord?
Is it thy ears that suffer, or thy heart?
CREON
Why seek to probe and find the seat of pain?
GUARD
I gall thine ears--this miscreant thy mind.
CREON
What an inveterate babbler! get thee gone!
GUARD
Babbler perchance, but innocent of the crime.
CREON
Twice guilty, having sold thy soul for gain.
GUARD
Alas! how sad when reasoners reason wrong.
CREON
Go, quibble with thy reason. If thou fail'st
To find these malefactors, thou shalt own
The wages of ill-gotten gains is death. (313-327)

Thought: Creon, irritated by the guard, threatens him with death. This is a far cry from the Creon we encountered in *Oedipus the King*.

CREON
Of all these Thebans none so deems but thou.
ANTIGONE
These think as I, but bate their breath to thee.
CREON

Hast thou no shame to differ from all these?
ANTIGONE
To reverence kith and kin can bring no shame. (506-512)

Thought: Emboldened by his power, Creon attempts to shame Antigone because her views are different from his.

CREON
Not even death can make a foe a friend.
ANTIGONE
My nature is for mutual love, not hate.
CREON
Die then, and love the dead if thou must;
No woman shall be the master while I live. (522-524)

Thought: Creon's power has made him arrogant and cold.

HAEMON
The Theban commons with one voice say, No.
CREON
What, shall the mob dictate my policy?
HAEMON
'Tis thou, methinks, who speakest like a boy.
CREON
Am I to rule for others, or myself?
HAEMON
A State for one man is no State at all.
CREON
The State is his who rules it, so 'tis held.
HAEMON
As monarch of a desert thou wouldst shine.
CREON
This boy, methinks, maintains the woman's cause.
HAEMON
If thou be'st woman, yes. My thought's for thee.
CREON
O reprobate, would'st wrangle with thy sire? (734-742)

Thought: Creon's power blinds him to the multitude of voices speaking against his actions.

TEIRESIAS
How far good counsel is the best of goods?
CREON
True, as unwisdom is the worst of ills.

TEIRESIAS
Thou art infected with that ill thyself.
CREON
I will not bandy insults with thee, seer.
TEIRESIAS
And yet thou say'st my prophesies are frauds.
CREON
Prophets are all a money-getting tribe.
TEIRESIAS
And kings are all a lucre-loving race.
CREON
Dost know at whom thou glancest, me thy lord?
TEIRESIAS
Lord of the State and savior, thanks to me. (1050-1058)

Thought: Having remarked just moments before that Teiresias's prophecies are always true, Creon attacks the man anyway when offended by what the prophet has to say. Here, Creon displays the same rashness and temper that Oedipus did as king, and against the same man.

Women and Femininity Quotes

ISMENE
Bethink thee, sister, of our father's fate,
Abhorred, dishonored, self-convinced of sin,
Blinded, himself his executioner.
Think of his mother-wife (ill sorted names)
Done by a noose herself had twined to death
And last, our hapless brethren in one day,
Both in a mutual destiny involved,
Self-slaughtered, both the slayer and the slain.
Bethink thee, sister, we are left alone;
Shall we not perish wretchedest of all,
If in defiance of the law we cross
A monarch's will?--weak women, think of that,
Not framed by nature to contend with men.
Remember this too that the stronger rules;
We must obey his orders, these or worse.
Therefore I plead compulsion and entreat
The dead to pardon. I perforce obey
The powers that be. 'Tis foolishness, I ween,
To overstep in aught the golden mean. (49-68)

Thought: Ismene argues that because she and Antigone are women, they lack the power to defy the state.

CREON
Elders, the gods have righted one again
Our storm-tossed ship of state, now safe in port.
But you by special summons I convened
As my most trusted councilors; first, because
I knew you loyal to Laius of old;
Again, when Oedipus restored our State,
Both while he ruled and when his rule was o'er,
Ye still were constant to the royal line.
Now that his two sons perished in one day,
Brother by brother murderously slain,
By right of kinship to the Princes dead,
I claim and hold the throne and sovereignty.
Yet 'tis no easy matter to discern
The temper of a man, his mind and will,
Till he be proved by exercise of power;
And in my case, if one who reigns supreme
Swerve from the highest policy, tongue-tied
By fear of consequence, that man I hold,
And ever held, the basest of the base.
And I contemn the man who sets his friend
Before his country. For myself, I call
To witness Zeus, whose eyes are everywhere,
If I perceive some mischievous design
To sap the State, I will not hold my tongue;
Nor would I reckon as my private friend
A public foe, well knowing that the State
Is the good ship that holds our fortunes all:
Farewell to friendship, if she suffers wreck.
Such is the policy by which I seek
To serve the Commons and conformably
I have proclaimed an edict as concerns
The sons of Oedipus; Eteocles
Who in his country's battle fought and fell,
The foremost champion--duly bury him
With all observances and ceremonies
That are the guerdon of the heroic dead.
But for the miscreant exile who returned
Minded in flames and ashes to blot out
His father's city and his father's gods,
And glut his vengeance with his kinsmen's blood,
Or drag them captive at his chariot wheels--
For Polyneices 'tis ordained that none
Shall give him burial or make mourn for him,
But leave his corpse unburied, to be meat
For dogs and carrion crows, a ghastly sight.
So am I purposed; never by my will

Shall miscreants take precedence of true men,
But all good patriots, alive or dead,
Shall be by me preferred and honored. (280-314)

Thought: Creon automatically assumes the law-breaker is a man.

CREON
Well, let her know the stubbornest of wills
Are soonest bended, as the hardest iron,
O'er-heated in the fire to brittleness,
Flies soonest into fragments, shivered through.
A snaffle curbs the fieriest steed, and he
Who in subjection lives must needs be meek.
But this proud girl, in insolence well-schooled,
First overstepped the established law, and then--
A second and worse act of insolence--
She boasts and glories in her wickedness.
Now if she thus can flout authority
Unpunished, I am woman, she the man.
But though she be my sister's child or nearer
Of kin than all who worship at my hearth,
Nor she nor yet her sister shall escape
The utmost penalty, for both I hold,
As arch-conspirators, of equal guilt.
Bring forth the older; even now I saw her
Within the palace, frenzied and distraught.
The workings of the mind discover oft
Dark deeds in darkness schemed, before the act.
More hateful still the miscreant who seeks
When caught, to make a virtue of a crime. (474-496)

Thought: Creon implies that men are the enforcers of law while women are weak and to be controlled.

CREON
Not even death can make a foe a friend.
ANTIGONE
My nature is for mutual love, not hate.
CREON
Die then, and love the dead if thou must;
No woman shall be the master while I live. (522-524)

Thought: Creon reveals that his reasoning is based on sexism, not on rationality.

CREON
What evils are not wrought by Anarchy!
She ruins States, and overthrows the home,
She dissipates and routs the embattled host;
While discipline preserves the ordered ranks.
Therefore we must maintain authority
And yield to title to a woman's will.
Better, if needs be, men should cast us out
Than hear it said, a woman proved his match. (671-680)

Thought: Creon attributes anarchy to women and feels strongly that a social structure favoring men must be maintained.

CREON
Play not the spaniel, thou a woman's slave.
HAEMON
When thou dost speak, must no man make reply? (754-755)

Thought: Creon insults Haemon by suggesting he is subservient to Antigone.

Mortality Quotes

ISMENE
To me, Antigone, no word of friends
Has come, or glad or grievous, since we twain
Were reft of our two brethren in one day
By double fratricide; and since i' the night
Our Argive leaguers fled, no later news
Has reached me, to inspirit or deject. (11-17)

Thought: Just as Oedipus's family was the cause of his self-injury, so his sons are the cause of each other's death.

I would not welcome such a fellowship.
Go thine own way; myself will bury him.
How sweet to die in such employ, to rest,--
Sister and brother linked in love's embrace--
A sinless sinner, banned awhile on earth,
But by the dead commended; and with them
I shall abide for ever. As for thee,
Scorn, if thou wilt, the eternal laws of Heaven. (69-76)

Thought: Antigone welcomes, and even loves, the idea of death. She is the only character to do so.

ANTIGONE
Sister, forbear, or I shall hate thee soon,
And the dead man will hate thee too, with cause.
Say I am mad and give my madness rein
To wreck itself; the worst that can befall
Is but to die an honorable death. (92-96)

Thought: Because Antigone approaches death without regret, her demise takes on a tone other than the tragic feel of Jocasta's suicide.

ANTIGONE
Would'st thou do more than slay thy prisoner?
CREON
Not I, thy life is mine, and that's enough.
ANTIGONE
Why dally then? To me no word of thine
Is pleasant: God forbid it e'er should please;
Nor am I more acceptable to thee.
And yet how otherwise had I achieved
A name so glorious as by burying
A brother? so my townsmen all would say,
Where they not gagged by terror, Manifold
A king's prerogatives, and not the least
That all his acts and all his words are law. (497-506)

Thought: Antigone's approach to death is not as fearless as she claims; unable to live in a world where divine law crumbles under human law, she finds death to be the only option left to her.

ANTIGONE
(Str. 1)
Friends, countrymen, my last farewell I make;
My journey's done.
One last fond, lingering, longing look I take
At the bright sun.
For Death who puts to sleep both young and old
Hales my young life,
And beckons me to Acheron's dark fold,
An unwed wife.
No youths have sung the marriage song for me,
My bridal bed

No maids have strewn with flowers from the lea,
'Tis Death I wed. (806-813)

Thought: Antigone imagines death as a marriage, establishing yet another duality in the play.

MESSENGER
So at the bidding of our distraught lord
We looked, and in the craven's vaulted gloom
I saw the maiden lying strangled there,
A noose of linen twined about her neck;
And hard beside her, clasping her cold form,
Her lover lay bewailing his dead bride
Death-wedded, and his father's cruelty.
When the King saw him, with a terrible groan
He moved towards him, crying, "O my son
What hast thou done? What ailed thee? What mischance
Has reft thee of thy reason? O come forth,
Come forth, my son; thy father supplicates."
But the son glared at him with tiger eyes,
Spat in his face, and then, without a word,
Drew his two-hilted sword and smote, but missed
His father flying backwards. Then the boy,
Wroth with himself, poor wretch, incontinent
Fell on his sword and drove it through his side
Home, but yet breathing clasped in his lax arms
The maid, her pallid cheek incarnadined
With his expiring gasps. So there they lay
Two corpses, one in death. His marriage rites
Are consummated in the halls of Death:
A witness that of ills whate'er befall
Mortals' unwisdom is the worst of all. (1192-2144)

Thought: For Eurydice, suicide becomes the only choice once she learns of the double deaths of Antigone and Haemon.

SECOND MESSENGER
Hearing the loud lament above her son
With her own hand she stabbed herself to the heart. (1316-1317)

Thought: Eurydice's death strangely parallels Jocasta's suicide, which was in response to the metaphorical death of her perception of Oedipus.

Plot Analysis

Classic Plot Analysis

Initial Situation
Antigone arrives in Thebes and finds that her brothers are dead, Polyneices's dead body is unburried, and there is a royal edict against burying him.
This is what's up at the beginning of the book. We even have a little bit of conflict right off the bat.

Conflict
Antigone wants to bury Polyneices even though it is against the law and asks Ismene for help. Ismene refuses.
Antigone discovers that if she's going to burry her brother, she's going to have to go it alone.

Complication
Antigone buries Polyneices, but is caught and brought to Creon. Antigone challenges Creon's decision and moral authority to prohibit the burial.
Antigone's situation gets worse. (You weren't supposed to disagree with the King. Ever.)

Climax
Creon sentences Antigone to death and locks her away.
We TOLD you you're not supposed to argue with the King. Antigone's fate is sealed.

Suspense
Haemon, Teiresias, and the Chorus all plead with Creon to let Antigone go.
Although Antigone seems destined to die, there is hope again that she will be released.

Denouement
Creon decides, grudgingly, to release Antigone.
Creon's reversal of his decision offers final hope to Antigone.

Conclusion
When Creon arrives to release Antigone, he finds that she, Haemon, and his wife have all killed themselves.
Creon's decision came too late. The play ends.

Booker's Seven Basic Plots Analysis: Tragedy

Anticipation Stage
Antigone returns to Thebes with the intention of helping her brothers avoid the prophecy of their death.
Antigone is hopeful and dedicated to serving her brothers. She is focused and confident.

Dream Stage
Antigone discovers her brothers are dead and that Polyneices has not been given a proper burial. She commits herself to burying her brother at all costs.
Antigone dreams of giving her brother a proper burial.

Frustration Stage
Antigone is caught burying her brother and is brought to Creon. She willingly admits her crime and further irritates Creon by challenging his moral authority.
Antigone defends her actions, and by further irritating Creon, essentially seals her fate. Well, for the time being at least.

Nightmare Stage
Antigone is locked away in a jail cell to die.
Locked away in jail, Antigone realizes that she's definitely going to die.

Destruction or Death Wish Stage
Antigone perceives her death as imminent and so commits suicide in jail. Finding her dead, Antigone's fiancé Haemon and Creon's wife kill themselves. Creon intends to release Antigone, but discovers them all dead instead. Much grief follows.
Unable to bear their circumstances any longer, the main characters all kill or injure themselves. This is sounding quite familiar.

Three Act Plot Analysis

Act I
Antigone learns that her brothers are dead and that Polyneices is unburied. She asks Ismene to break the law with her and bury him. When Ismene refuses, she goes it alone.

Act II
Antigone successfully buries her brother but is caught. Antigone refuses to allow Ismene to accept any blame for the crime she did not commit. Antigone challenges Creon's moral authority and he sentences her to death.

Act III
Antigone is locked away. Haemon, Teiresias, and the Chorus plead with Creon to spare her. Creon grudgingly agrees to let her off, but discovers that she has killed herself. Her fiancé (Haemon) and Creon's wife commit suicide as well. Creon is in despair.

Study Questions

1. How are women portrayed in *Antigone*?

2. Discuss the conflict between fate and destiny on one hand and free will on the other. Which dominates? How does each character grapple with their limited free will?
3. How do the play's main characters (Creon, Antigone, Ismene) see themselves? How is this similar or different from how they are perceived by others?
4. What function does off-stage action have in *Antigone*? Why, for example, does Sophocles sometimes have messengers describe actions that have occurred rather than portraying events directly?
5. Compare and contrast Oedipus and Antigone. How are they similar? Different?
6. Antigone assumed her fate was to die in jail and therefore killed herself, fulfilling her fate only because she was aware of it. The question is, if characters were not aware of their own supposed fate, would it be fulfilled? Or, for those of you who've seen *The Matrix*, would Neo still have broken the vase if the Oracle hadn't said anything

Characters

All Characters

Antigone Character Analysis

Family Loyalty

Antigone is a no-nonsense kind of woman. She first appears at the end of Oedipus the King as a little girl. Sophocles doesn't give her any lines, but her presence seems to be symbolic of the legacy of shame caused by Oedipus's horrific mistakes. Oedipus laments the life of humiliation that his daughters will have to lead. Ironically, he also gets Creon to promise to take care of his daughters. (So much for promises.)

Oedipus at Colonus is also graced with Antigone's presence. In this play, we see that she's become her father's devoted companion in exile. Once Oedipus dies, Antigone has to find someone else to be blindly loyal to (pun intended). So, she heads back to Thebes where she can support her brothers, Polyneices and Eteocles.

In *Antigone* Antigone gets promoted to protagonist. It's not a job we would want; Sophocles' protagonists always fall and fall hard. They don't call them tragic heroines for nothing. Antigone's fate seems to be sealed even from the prologue. We learn that her brothers have killed each other in a war over their father's throne. Creon, the new king, declares that the body of Eteocles will be honored, but that Polyneices's corpse will be left to rot. Anyone who attempts to bury Polyneices will be executed.

Antigone's fierce devotion is once more on full display when she declares that she'll bury

Polyneices despite Creon's law. It is this rebellious act and Antigone's determined loyalty to the memory of her brother that forms the spine of the play. Her stubborn loyalty becomes her *hamartia*, her tragic error, and ultimately causes her downfall. Antigone is a great example of how a *hamartia* doesn't necessarily have to be a character "flaw" as it is often described. Most people would call loyalty an admirable trait. Antigone's devotion is so extreme, however, that it brings tragedy once more to Thebes.

You probably noticed that "loyalty" is a big word when it comes to Antigone. Family devotion especially is a big thing. She sacrifices her own life in the name of it. Her determination is so strong that her character becomes symbolic of family loyalty or blood ties. When we see her clash with King Creon, it's almost as if Sophocles is asking: "Who do we owe more loyalty to? The government or our families?" It's not a hard question for Antigone to answer, but it might not be as clear cut as you think.

Imagine if you will: a top American general has allied himself with terrorists and attacked the U.S., killing millions. The general died in the battle and the U.S. government has declared that anyone attempting to bury him will be put to death. What would you do if this general was one of your family members? Risk life and limb just because you were related? Even if you were really close to the person, would you go against the government's wishes?

Loyalty to the Gods

Antigone's other big thing is her fierce loyalty to the gods. Their divine laws are what she holds most sacred. She couldn't give a flip about laws of man, as represented by Creon. When these two willful characters collide, the clash isn't just symbolic of government vs. family; it's also symbolic of man vs. the gods.

Throughout the play there are signs in the natural world that the gods are on the side of Antigone. For one, there are no footprints left beside the body when Antigone first puts dust on Polyneices. It's as if the earth itself is attempting to aid Antigone in her "crime." When the Sentry reports this strange phenomenon, the Chorus asks Creon if it might be the gods' work. The King dismisses the idea, saying the gods wouldn't want to help out somebody as terrible as Polyneices. (Boy, is Creon wrong.)

We also see divine support for Antigone, when the storm rages outside of Thebes. The Sentry and friends go back to Polyneices's body and wipe away the soil that Antigone sprinkled there. No sooner do they do this than the dust erupts from the earth and blots out the sky. In the center of the storm stands Antigone, wailing for the gods to destroy whoever has re-desecrated Polyneices's body. Seems like a pretty clear sign that Creon had better watch his back.

Antigone's divine symbolism is also seen when she is dragged before Creon just after the Chorus's famous "Ode to Man." There's more on this in the Chorus's "Character Analysis," but basically the Chorus has just gotten done singing a song about how awesome man is for conquering nature and how no one should step to our mighty laws. As soon as they're done singing, Antigone is hauled in. It's almost as if Antigone is the gods' answer to the Chorus's overweening pride. She is like a Fury, the gods' tool for revenge.

Girl Power

Antigone is also a symbol of feminine revolt. She's nowhere near as radical as Euripides' Medea, who assassinates the royal family and murders her own children in the name of women. However, Antigone sacrifices her own life, trying to stand up to the patriarchal society in which she's imprisoned. You can look at Antigone's clash with Creon as symbolic of the larger struggle of man vs. woman.

Ismene warns Antigone in the prologue that they are just weak women and can't stand up to the men-folk. Antigone proceeds anyway. When Antigone argues that her actions were justified by her loyalty to her family and to the gods, Creon dismisses her as an overemotional woman. Antigone barely gives this notion the time of day, and stands before her accuser unrepentant.

It's interesting that though Antigone is definitely a feminist symbol, she's spent her life being dutiful to men. Her childhood was spent following Oedipus around. Now she's giving her life for her fallen brother. We wonder if, even though she's a strong independent woman, she needs these male presences for emotional sustenance. We also notice how cold she is with her sister Ismene. Could it be that Antigone is a woman-hating woman? Maybe, maybe not. What's your take?

In Love with Death?

Why is Antigone so fearless? Interestingly, she seems empowered by her feeling that she'll be cursed no matter what. Basically, Antigone has nothing to lose. This ship is going down. At times, she even expresses a seeming fervor to die. As she's led to her tomb, she characterizes Death, not Haemon, as her future husband. She describes her tomb as a bridal chamber. Though she also expresses fear, she definitely seems to be a little in love with death. Perhaps, it's because she's been around such tragedy all her life. Maybe, she's weary of her cursed, obligation-ridden life and just wants to return to her father and brothers. What do you think?

Antigone Timeline and Summary

- At the beginning of *Antigone*, Antigone and her sister Ismene return to Thebes in an attempt to help their brothers. The sisters learn that both of their brothers are dead.
- Antigone asks Ismene to help her bury her brother Polyneices, whom Creon has refused to allow to be buried. Ismene says the danger is too substantial and that they will not succeed. Antigone disagrees. She feels it's morally imperative and within their power. She decides to act alone.
- Antigone performs the burial rites, but is caught in the act.
- A sentry brings Antigone to Creon.
- Creon attempts to humiliate Antigone but is unsuccessful. She confesses quickly, and willingly accepts and even welcomes death.
- Antigone refuses to allow Ismene to take any blame for the crime.
- Creon locks Antigone away.
- Antigone hangs herself in prison.

Creon Character Analysis

Antagonist Not Villain

Creon shows up in all three of Sophocles' Theban plays. He goes through quite a transformation over the course of the story. In *Oedipus the King*, he seems like a totally rational guy. His cool reason highlights Oedipus's hot temper. In *Oedipus at Colonus* he becomes the full-fledged smooth-talker he had in him all along. He attempts to sugarcoat his plea for Oedipus to return to Thebes, and could be seen as cowardly and weak when he kidnaps Oedipus's daughters.

By the time *Antigone* rolls around, Creon, the play's antagonist, has become an absolute tyrant. His hyper-logical mind refuses to recognize the bonds of familial love that tie Antigone to her brother Polyneices. He rejects the irrational laws of the gods in favor the rational laws of man. It's interesting that the cool reason that seemed like such a good thing in *Oedipus the King* now causes his downfall. Hmm, we detect the distinct scent of Sophocles' favorite dish: tragic irony.

One of the things that sets great tragedy apart from mere melodrama is that all the characters ultimately have good intentions. The plays become tragically ironic when these good intentions bring misery and horror for all. Though, it's easy to pigeon-hole Creon as a big mean man, persecuting his brave, innocent niece, it's just not that simple. In great tragedy, there are antagonists (like Creon) but there are rarely villains.

Lawmaker

The first thing Creon does in *Antigone* is declare a harsh but understandable law. He proclaims that while the body of Eteocles will be buried with dignity, the corpse of Polyneices will be left to rot on the field of battle. Anyone who attempts to honor Polyneices's body with burial will be sentenced to death. Sure, it's not the nicest law, but think about this: Polyneices is a traitor. He allied with other city-states and attacked his hometown. He nearly brought on the whole sale destruction of Thebes.

Of course, Polyneices only led this attack because his brother Eteocles refused to share the throne as they had agreed. Still, many Thebans have lost fathers, brothers, and sons, because of Polyneices's assault. In the *parados* the Chorus expresses anger at Polyneices and joy over his defeat, showing that the people of Thebes are none too pleased with his actions. The people, represented by the Chorus, seem to support Creon's decree.

Here's a hypothetical, similar to the one we pose in Antigone's "Character Analysis" : what would happen today if one of America's top generals allied himself with terrorists and led an attack on the U.S.? If such a person died in the battle would they be buried with full honors in Arlington? The president would have a really hard time justifying such an action. Sure the body would be allowed burial somewhere, but still (just as in ancient Thebes) the traitorous soldier's remains would most likely be in some way symbolically dishonored.

Obstinate or Steadfast?
Though Creon's first law as king isn't totally unreasonable, it does turn out to be a really, REALLY bad idea. Creon makes matters worse by refusing to relent in the face of mounting opposition. His tenacious allegiance to the laws of state turns out to be his *hamartia*, a word commonly referred to as tragic flaw, but more accurately translated as tragic error.

It's interesting that we see him behaving much the way Oedipus does in *Oedipus the King*. Ironically, Creon starts accusing everybody of conspiracy, just the way Oedipus accused him. Also like Oedipus, he disbelieves the words of the blind prophet Teiresias. When the seer predicts that Creon's course of action will result in the death of Creon's whole family, the paranoid king accuses the seer of having been bribed.

Once again, though, what seems to be a flaw is also in some ways a virtue. Creon's fierce dedication to law and order seems to be exactly what Thebes needs. The city is just coming back together from a state of total anarchy. The people need a strong and steadfast leader to bring them together. How's it going to look if Creon goes against the very first law he makes? Creon's concern for his public image is certainly in some ways self-motivated. He doesn't want to get punked down, especially by a woman. However, this seemingly selfish worry also comes out of a concern for his people. A wishy-washy leader can be a very dangerous thing in a time of crisis. If Creon appears to be weak the whole city could descend back into chaos.

Also notice that Creon isn't totally dogmatic about his decree. Slowly, over the course of the play he becomes less and less extreme. First he relents on having Ismene executed along with her sister. Next he has Antigone entombed instead of outright executed. In the end, he is ultimately convinced by Teiresias's prediction and goes to release Antigone. Unfortunately, he's a little too late. Before he can stop it, his niece, his son, and his wife have all committed suicide. At the play's conclusion, Creon's downfall becomes symbolic of the tragedies that occur when the laws of man attempt to compete with the ancient laws of the gods.

For more Creon check out *Oedipus the King* and *Oedipus at Colonus*.

Creon Timeline and Summary

- After Eteocles and Polyneices kill each other, Creon takes the throne of Thebes.
- Creon orders that, because Polyneices attacked the city, he will not be given proper burial rites. Anyone who buries Polyneices will be punished by death.
- Creon learns from a sentry that someone has buried Polyneices.
- Creon demands that the sentry discover who did it. He threatens the sentry with death if he can't figure it out.
- The sentry brings Antigone in and reports that she was the one who buried Polyneices. Creon vows to execute her.
- Creon and Antigone argue over the virtue of the law.

- Creon discuses with his son Haemon his decision to have Antigone executed.
- Teiresias arrives to speak with Creon. He advises Creon not to execute Antigone, because possibly (although he doesn't say this directly) EVERYONE will die.
- When Creon refuses to obey the prophet, Teiresias predicts he will suffer and die. This part IS quite direct.
- Creon grapples with his choices. At the Chorus's urging, he goes to release Antigone and see to Polyneices's burial.
- Before he can release Antigone, Creon discovers that his wife, Antigone, and Haemon have killed themselves.
- In despair and fear of his own death, Creon asks to be led off stage.

Teiresias Character Analysis

Teiresias is kind of a cranky old fellow. We can see why. Though he's blind, he can see better than any of those around him. He's in tune with the mind of Apollo and receives visions of the future. Teiresias is also gifted in the magic art of augury, or telling the future from the behavior of birds. You might think these are pretty awesome skills, but it probably really stinks when everybody around you is doomed to shame, death, or mutilation. It's probably especially annoying that whenever Teiresias does drop a little knowledge, people don't believe him. In *Oedipus the King*, Jocasta and Oedipus are both skeptical of his prophecies. Oedipus even goes so far as to accuse Teiresias of conspiring against him with Creon.

When Teiresias shambles on stage in *Antigone*, he once again gets accused of being a traitor. Ironically this time it's Creon that accuses the prophet, saying that Teiresias must have been bribed. Creon just can't accept it when Teiresias tells him that nature itself is rebelling against Creon's double sacrilege. The gods of the heavens and the earth are angered by the fact that he has kept a dead man from being rightfully buried and has entombed a living girl. Creon's obstinately rational mind can't accept Teiresias's irrational argument. The conflict between the king and the prophet echoes the conflict between Creon and Antigone. Once again we see the laws of man butting heads with the ancient laws of the gods.

When Creon refuses to give in, Teiresias drops the knowledge that Creon's own family will die as a result of his blasphemous actions. Before Creon can reply to news of this dark prophecy, Teiresias exits the stage. If the seer had stuck around he would've seen that his words do in fact move Creon. Along with the urging of the Chorus, Creon quickly runs off to try and avert oncoming tragedy. Of course, maybe Teiresias doesn't stick around because he knows how it's all going to turn out. Just like Sophocles' ancient audience, he's heard this story before.

Do you want all Teiresias all the time? Then check out Sophocles' *Oedipus the King*.

Teiresias Timeline and Summary

* In *Antigone*, when Creon is king, Teiresias shows up to warn Creon about the potential consequences of his decision to leave Polyneices unburied and to execute Antigone.
* When Creon disregards and insults him, Teiresias remarks that no one seems able to listen and hear good advice.

Ismene Character Analysis

Ismene is Antigone Lite. She first puts in an appearance along with her sister at the end of Oedipus the King. Both girls seem to be symbolic of the legacy of shame left by Oedipus's mistakes. In *Oedipus at Colonus*, Ismene shows great loyalty to her father when she alerts him to the situation with Creon. She shows devotion once more when she returns with Antigone to Thebes. In *Antigone*, however, we see that Ismene's loyalty only extends so far. Though she agrees morally with Antigone's decision to bury Polyneices, she is afraid to risk her own life.

Like her sister, Ismene seems to value family ties and the laws of the gods over the laws of man. However, she's just not gutsy enough to stand up for her beliefs. The courage to stand beside her sister does eventually come to Ismene. When Creon arrests both daughters of Oedipus, Ismene asks that she be executed alongside Antigone. Antigone, however, scorns Ismene's belated attempt at righteousness. At the urging of the Chorus, Creon eventually relents on executing Ismene. The girl ends the play with her life intact, but her self-worth in shreds.

Before we close the book on Ismene, we'd just like to recognize that the strong will that her sister is often praised for is also the thing that causes three suicides. If Antigone were a bit more like her sister, this wouldn't be a tragedy at all. Ismene's argument at the beginning of the play is that their family has suffered enough. What's the point of bringing more sorrow? Antigone and Ismene have had to live with the stigma Oedipus's horrific mistakes their whole lives. To top it all off, their two beloved brothers have just murdered each other. We can see Ismene's point. Is Ismene really that bad for just wanting to finally live in peace?

Ismene Timeline and Summary

* Ismene and Antigone return to Thebes in order to try to prevent their brothers from killing each other. They are too late, however, and learn that their brothers are dead.
* Antigone asks Ismene to help her illegally bury their brother Polyneices.
* Ismene says she cannot act against the law and that she fears the consequences.
* After Antigone acts alone and is caught, Ismene attempts to accept part of the blame. However, Antigone refuses to let her.

The Chorus Character Analysis

The Function of the Chorus

The Chorus is roughly like the peanut-gallery. In *Antigone* the Chorus is made up of a group of old Theban men. They're probably old men because most of the young ones have just died in battle. Also, they represent in some way the deeply embedded patriarchal (male dominated) society that Antigone defies.

In *Antigone* the Chorus at times directly affects the action of the play. Though they at first seem to be totally on the side of their new king Creon, they begin to urge him to be more moderate. It's at their pleading that Creon decides not to sentence Ismene to death along with her sister. The old men of Thebes also practically insist that Creon take Teiresias's advice and free Antigone. Creon, of course, finally agrees to do this, but unfortunately it's far too late.

The main functions of the Chorus are to comment on the action of the play, give back story, and to connect the play to other myths. Sophocles also uses the Chorus to expound upon the play's central themes. In *Antigone* we get choral odes on everything from the triumph of man over nature, to the dangers of pride, to the hazards of love.

Parodos

As in every ancient Greek tragedy, the first time we hear the Chorus is when they sing their *parados* or entry song. *Parados* looks a little bit like the modern word "parade," right? This is probably no accident. When the Chorus performed the parados they would "parade" in, singing and dancing with much fanfare. The actual word "parados" comes from the name of the corridor or archway through which the Chorus first entered.

In *Antigone*, Sophocles uses the *parados* to give back-story. The Chorus sings all about the terrible battle that has just been fought. We also get the sense that the people of Thebes are furious at Polyneices for betraying and attacking them. This helps to strengthen Creon's position about the traitor's burial.

Overall, the *parados* in *Antigone* is a joyful celebration of victory. This is, of course, highly ironic. The audience has just watched the prologue, in which Antigone declares her intentions to defy the state. Though Thebes has just defeated an external enemy, the new order represented by Creon will be challenged almost immediately by an enemy from within.

"Ode to Man"

The next time we hear the Chorus is the First Ode. This little ditty just happens to be the most famous choral ode in all of Greek tragedy. It is popularly referred to as the "Ode to Man." In this celebrated ode the Chorus sings about all the wonderful accomplishments of man. The word "wonderful" in Greek is *deinon*. It can also describe something that is terrible. In a way, the word means both wonderful and terrible at the same time. But how could all of man's accomplishments be both of those things at once?

Let's take a look at the achievements that the Chorus lists. Humanity has: built ships to conquer the seas, crafted plows to tame the earth, bent animals to his will, raised houses to defeat the rain and the snow. Do you notice a common thread here? Nearly everything is about humanity asserting its will over nature. This echoes the basic conflict of the play.

Creon represents the state or man-made civilization. Antigone represents the primal will of the gods, a.k.a. nature. The storm outside of Thebes and the auguries of Teiresias hint that nature is offended by Creon's actions and stands on the side of Antigone. When all of Creon's family members kill themselves by the end of the play, it's as if nature itself is taking payment for his sacrilege. In a way, all of man's accomplishments could be seen as being just as terrible as they are wonderful. Each time we take a step forward, we separate ourselves father from the place that we began.

The Chorus ends the "Ode to Man" by praising the laws of the city. They disdain anybody who would want to bring anarchy back to Thebes. After the ode concludes, it takes Sophocles about two seconds to lather on the irony. Who should show up in chains just as soon as Chorus gets done talking junk about anarchists? Why it's Antigone – everyone's favorite protagonist and anarchist extraordinaire. When Antigone appears just as the "Ode to Man" concludes it's almost as if she's the god's answer to the great *hubris* (pride) shown in the Chorus's song.

Other Odes

Sophocles uses the second choral ode to relate the tragic history of Oedipus's family. This ode complements the scene before in which Ismene attempts to go to her death along with her sister Antigone. In the third choral ode the Chorus sings of the hazards of love. This is a comment on the previous scene where Haimon begs for the life of his beloved Antigone. The fourth ode gives the audience some trivia about other mythic figures who've been entombed. The tone of the terrible tales in this ode seem to show that Chorus is beginning to really pity Antigone. By the end of the play the Chorus has totally changed their tune. These same old men who were previously celebrating man's mastery over nature are humbled in the face of the gods.

Strophe, Antistrophe

Like most all ancient Greek tragedians, Sophocles divides his choral odes into strophe and antistrophe. Both sections had the same number of lines and metrical pattern. In Greek, *strophe* means "turn," and *antistrophe* means "turn back." This makes sense when you consider the fact that, during the strophe choruses danced from right to left and during the antistrophe they did the opposite. Sophocles may have split them into two groups, so that it was as if one part of the Chorus was conversing with the other. Perhaps the dualities created by strophe and antistrophe, represent the endless irresolvable debates for which Greek tragedy is famous.

The Chorus Timeline and Summary

- Note: Although they pipe up only once in a while, the Chorus is present throughout the entire action of the play as an observer.
- Upon learning that someone buried Polyneices, the Chorus chimes in that perhaps the

burial was the will of the gods. Creon angrily responds that Polyneices spited the gods with his actions.
- The Chorus comments on the strength and resilience of mankind.
- Upon learning that Antigone buried Polyneices, the Chorus accuses her of being inclined to trouble like her father.
- The Chorus laments life's sufferings.
- The Chorus tries to dissuade Creon from punishing Ismene, who clearly did not participate in Polyneices's burial.
- Teiresias leaves, after offering his advice to Creon, and the Chorus reminds Creon that Teiresias is never wrong.
- Creon is swayed by the Chorus's urging to release Antigone and see to Polyneices's burial.
- The Chorus concludes quite happily that man can't escape his doomed fate, but that hopefully we get smarter as we get older.

Character Roles

Protagonist

Antigone

Antigone is the most likely candidate for protagonist of *Antigone*. There is actually a bit of debate about this. Creon gets way more stage time and goes through a more distinct character arc, which leads some to argue that he's the real protagonist. The best case for Creon as protagonist lies in the fact that he is the one that experiences Aristotle's concepts of *peripeteia* and *anagnorisis*. Both of these were important elements for a tragic hero or heroine to have.

The *peripeteia* is a reversal of fortune. Creon certainly experiences this. The tragic events of the play transform him from a pillar of pride into a puddle of humility. After his downfall he experiences *anagnorisis* or a recognition. He realizes the law he passed was a really bad idea and regrets his pride. Antigone on the other hand, knows exactly what is going to happen to her from the beginning of the play and never regrets a thing.

So, yes, there's a really good argument for Creon as protagonist, but check this out. Antigone is the one who drives the action of the play. She is the one who sets the tragedy into motion. She is the one who buries Polyneices despite Creon's strict edict. It is Antigone's suicide that causes her fiancé Haemon to stab himself, which in turn cause's Creon's wife Eurydice to commit suicide. Also, it certainly seems like we're supposed to be sympathizing with her toward the end of the play, not Creon. The king himself comes over to her point of view. There's room for some friendly debate here, but it seems to us that Antigone is the center of the storm.

Antagonist

Creon

If Antigone is the protagonist that means Creon has got to be the antagonist. He's the force that Antigone goes up against. As we discuss above, there are some that see him as a possible protagonist. There are good reasons for this point of view, the best of these being that Creon is the one who has moments of *peripeteia* and *anagnorisis.*

We'd just like to point out, however, that it is Antigone not Creon who disturbs the world by breaking her uncle's law. Antigone drives the action, while Creon only reacts. He is constantly trying to rebuff Antigone's forward motion, rather than creating any of his own. This in our mind makes him seem like the most likely antagonist. Once again, there's room for debate. *Antigone* just doesn't fit snuggly into all of Aristotle's ideas.

Foil

Antigone to Oedipus

Antigone definitely has a lot of similarities to her father Oedipus. The Chorus even directly points this out. Just like Oedipus she is obstinate, proud, and endlessly determined. Also, like Oedipus she has the ability to make quick and decisive decisions. Unfortunately she is also similar to her father in that these seemingly positive traits lead to her ultimate destruction. Just like Oedipus, her choices bring about her downfall.

Though they are similar, the two characters are also foils. They differ on a crucial point. While Oedipus shows disdain for prophecy, his daughter shows great devotion to the will of the gods. Perhaps she learned this from watching his downfall. Of course, this lesson doesn't seem to do her any good. It is her unrelenting devotion to the laws of the gods which causes her death. It is ironic that Oedipus and his daughter go down, for what could be seen as the exact opposite reasons.

Foil

Antigone to Creon

Antigone and Creon are vastly different characters. The conflict between the two becomes symbolic of female vs. male, family vs. government, and gods vs. man. This is all discussed in their "Character Analyses." The only thing that seems to be similar about the two characters is their stubbornness. When two such determined people collide there's bound to be tragedy.

Foil

Antigone to Ismene

In a sense, Antigone and Ismene are foils. While Antigone demonstrates power and control over her own fate, Ismene shows weakness and the inability to take her life into her own hands. Ismene, unlike her sister, constantly gives in to the stronger wills around her.

Character Clues

Actions

Because *Antigone* is a play, Sophocles relies most heavily on action to characterize the players. Antigone, for example, demonstrates loyalty and devotion to her family and the gods by burying her brother even though it's against the law.

Speech

Dialogue is an extremely important means of characterization in *Antigone* because, as a play, the thoughts and opinions of characters are conveyed largely through speech. Creon is portrayed as arrogant because of the tone he uses when speaking to the prophet Teiresias. Antigone is depicted as strong and willful when she argues with Creon. The way in which characters speak (such as meekly or authoritatively) reflects both their status and confidence.

Whimsical and Reflective: The Chorus
The Chorus tends to muse over broad topics such as human nature, life and death. It speaks with a reflective and sometimes a foreboding tone.

Authoritative: Creon, Antigone, Teiresias
Most of the central characters in *Antigone* are determined and strong. Their strength is reflected in their use of authoritative language.

Intimidated, Shy, and Indecisive: Messengers, Ismene
A few characters stand out for speaking less authoritatively than others. Intimidated by strong characters such as Creon, the messengers and the shepherd speak very cautiously. Ismene's frailty, too, is reflected in her indecisive speech, especially in contrast to Antigone.

Direct Characterization
The qualities of each player are further explored by the commentary of the Chorus. The two halves of the Chorus, the Strophe and Antistrophe, for example, debate the strengths and weaknesses of Oedipus and Creon and by doing so, highlight characteristics of the two kings.

Literary Devices

Symbols, Imagery, Allegory

The Characters
Much of the symbolism in *Antigone* lies in the characters themselves. Antigone and Creon represent a number of opposing forces: male vs. female, family ties vs. civic duty, man vs. nature, and man's laws vs. the laws of the gods. Also, there's the blind prophet Teiresias who could be seen as representing the will of the gods. Check out the "Character Analysis" section for more details on the larger symbolism of the characters.

Entombment
Images of tombs and burials pop up a lot in the *Oedipus* plays. In *Antigone*, Creon causes all kinds of problems by bungling issues of burial. The prideful king has committed a double blasphemy by letting Polyneices's body go unburied, while entombing Antigone when she's still alive. At points we feel like saying, "No, no, Creon. It's the dead ones that go in the ground." The symbolic paradox of Creon's double blasphemy, shows just how far from sensible Creon's hubris has taken him.

Also, Antigone's fearless march to her own entombment and talk of being a bride to death suggests that she feels closer to her dead family members than to the living. She seems to have no problem at all leaving behind her sister Ismene and her fiancé Haemon, but talks of how swell it will be to reunite with Oedipus and her brothers in death. When Antigone takes her own life inside her tomb, it could be seen as symbolic of the fact that she's found the tragic fate she always knew awaited her.

Birds
There's tons of bird imagery throughout *Antigone*. For one, there's lots of talk of carrion birds making a buffet of Polyneices. The Chorus also describes Polyneices himself as a bird, a big mean eagle wreaking havoc on Thebes. This description seems to heighten the idea of Polyneices as fearful aggressor against his home town. The Chorus even goes so far as to describe Polyneices the eagle as feasting on their blood. This becomes pretty ironic when the birds are feasting on him.

Another instance of avian imagery is when the Sentry describes Antigone as hovering over Poyneices's body like a mother bird. Here the bird reference seems to strengthen Antigone's symbolism as both a maternal figure as well as representative of the ancient force of nature.

The biggest bit of bird symbolism comes from Teiresias. This is not a surprise, since the prophet is skilled in the magic art of augury or telling the future from the behavior of birds. The seer tells King Creon all about how the birds are fighting each other, which symbolizes the horrible imbalance the King has created in nature. Teiresias goes on to tell Creon that the birds won't talk about the future because they've gorged themselves on Polyneices's blood. (Yuck.) The birds have evidently also pooped all over the altars of Thebes. (A bad day for the altar cleaner.) All this foul bird imagery (pun intended!) seems to symbolize the corruption that Creon has caused by not burying Polyneices.

Setting

In Front of the Palace, Thebes, Ancient Greece
Antigone, like Oedipus the King, is set in that disaster-prone city-state known as Thebes. Though most Greek playwrights were from Athens, their plays are hardly ever set there. This is not because they had no hometown pride. In fact, they weren't allowed to set their plays in Athens. It seems Athenians preferred a little objective distance when examining tragedy. Though the plays were set in other places than Athens, they did take on hot-button Athenian issues. For example in *Antigone* the clash between Creon and Antigone can be seen as symbolic of the many cultural clashes going on in Athens at the time.

Probably the most prominent Athenian culture clash we see in *Antigone* is the laws of the state vs. religious fundamentalism. Sophocles was a religious conservative and was a member of several cults. However, in his time, a group called the Sophists was on the rise. These men valued rationality over what they thought of as superstition. Any Athenian even moderately aware of current events wouldn't have missed the warning encoded in Sophocles' play. When Creon, the hyper-rational representative of law and order falls to the will of the gods, it's pretty clear where Sophocles stood on this hot-button issue.

Athenians also liked objective distance in terms of time. Tragedies were almost always set in Greece's distant past. Sophocles and his buddies adapted their stories from the Greeks' rich oral tradition. These tales of gods and heroes had been handed down for generations. Antigone was an ancient figure even to the ancient Greeks.

Most specifically the play is set in front of the palace of Thebes. This place has been the sight of much tragedy for Antigone's family. It's where her mother/grandmother, Jocasta, committed suicide, and where her brother/father Oedipus discovered his shame and gouged out his own eyes. Not to mention the fact that the palace represents the throne that her brothers have just killed each other over. There's really no more fitting place for Antigone to receive her own tragic fate.

Genre

Tragedy
Antigone is one of the more famous tragedies ever to be written. Sophocles' play has served as a model for countless other playwrights over the years. Interestingly, though, it does differ from the model that Aristotle sets out in his tragic how-to manual *Poetics.*

As we talk about in our "Character Roles" section, *Antigone* differs from Aristotle's model in that it is the antagonist, Creon, who experiences *peripeteia* and *anagnorisis*. This leads some to believe that he's the real tragic hero here instead of his niece. Some people even argue that they both are tragic heroes. The lack of agreement on this key issue makes it pretty clear that the play doesn't fit all that neatly into Aristotle's definition.

The play does, however, meet Aristotle's other criteria. The action of the play has universal ramifications. The characters are of proper stature for tragedy. Both Creon and Antigone are of noble birth and both fall hard in the play. Both characters have a *hamartia*, a tragic error or flaw. With both Antigone and her uncle, their immense stubbornness and pride bring about their downfall.

Antigone like Oedipus the King also has the distinct cause and effect that Aristotle so admired. Each event brings on the next. The action of the play is a neat and orderly progression to catastrophe.

Tone

Tragic, Sympathetic, Foreboding, Ironic
It's important to know Sophocles didn't make the whole Oedipus story up. The myths had been around, so Sophocles's audience would have been familiar with the tragic ending before

the play began. This has a distinct impact on the tone of the plays. The actions of the characters take on a sense of irony and foreboding in this context.

Because the play doesn't have a narrator, the tone is profoundly shaped by the commentary of the Chorus. The Chorus expresses genuine sympathy for the situations of the characters, yet at the same time is acutely aware of the upcoming events.

What's Up With the Title?

Well, the title is rather self-explanatory. Antigone is the heroine of this play.

Did You Know?

Steaminess Rating

G

Although Antigone and her siblings are the product of an incestuous relationship (her father, Oedipus, accidentally married his mother), there is absolutely no sex in *Antigone*.

Best of the Web

Movie or TV Productions

Antigoni (1961)
http://www.imdb.com/title/tt0055375/
A movie version of the play in Greek.

Antigone (1984)
http://www.imdb.com/title/tt0086905/
A TV movie with Juliet Stevenson as Antigone.

Videos

Movie Clip
http://www.youtube.com/watch?v=FJyAQf2KfKk
A scene from the 1961 film.

Movie Clip
http://www.youtube.com/watch?v=lGT24uYPb2Y&feature=related
A scene from the 1984 TV movie.

Websites

Free E-Book of the *Oedipus* Plays
http://www.gutenberg.org/etext/31
This is the translation quoted by Shmoop. It was by Francis Storr.

13060642R00026

Printed in Great Britain
by Amazon.co.uk, Ltd.,
Marston Gate.